Piano Accompaniment

# EASY CHRISTMAS CAROLS
# Instrumental Solos

Arranged by Bill Galliford, Ethan Neuburg and Tod Edmondson



ISBN-10: 0-7390-8403-8
ISBN-13: 978-0-7390-8403-8

# Contents

# AWAY IN A MANGER (MEDLEY)

Music by
JAMES R. MURRAY (1887) and
WILLIAM J. KIRKPATRICK

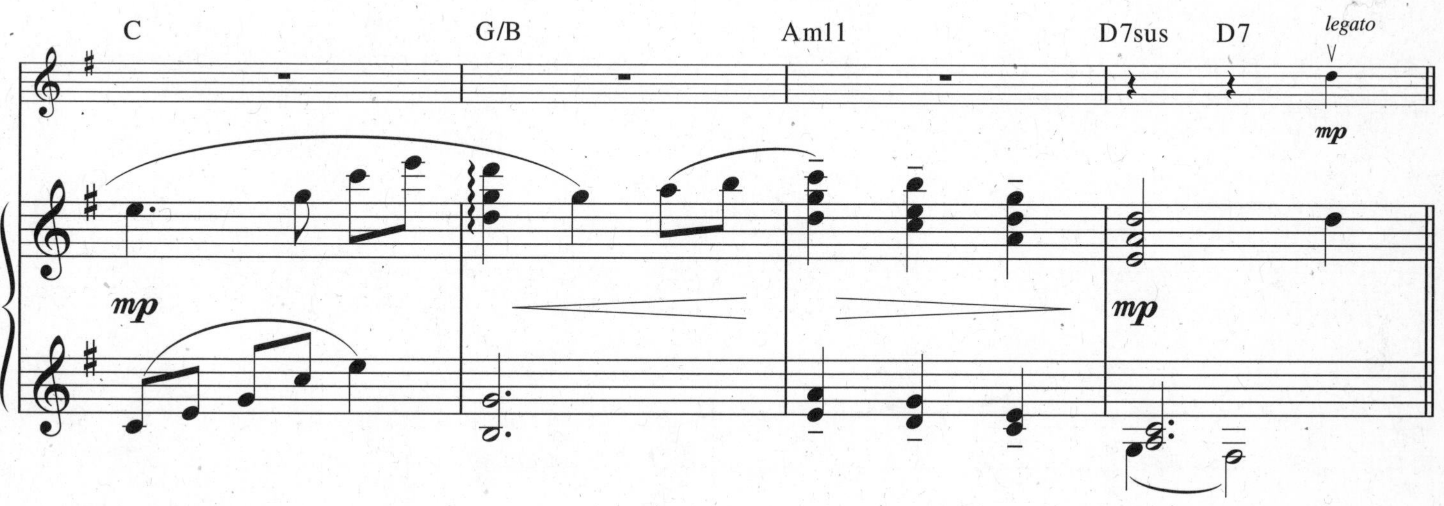

Gsus D/G C/G G Cmaj7 G/B Am7

G G+ Cmaj7 Bm7 G/B

Am7 D/F# G D/F# Em7 Am/G D7 G

C G/B Am11 D7sus D7

*mf*

*mp*

## "Away in a Manger (Cradle Song)"

29 Music by WILLIAM J. KIRKPATRICK

45
Em
Bm7/D
Cmaj7
G(9)/B
8va
E♭
B♭/D
Cm7
Dsus
mf
54
D
G2
p
8va
Am/G
(8va)
G2
A7/G

D7/G G Dm7/G G

(8va)

C Am D7 G/B

mf

mf

70

Am7 D7 Am7/G G C2

mp

mp

G(9)/B C/E D/F♯ G(9)

rit. p

rit. p

pp

8vb

# ANGELS WE HAVE HEARD ON HIGH

Traditional French Melody

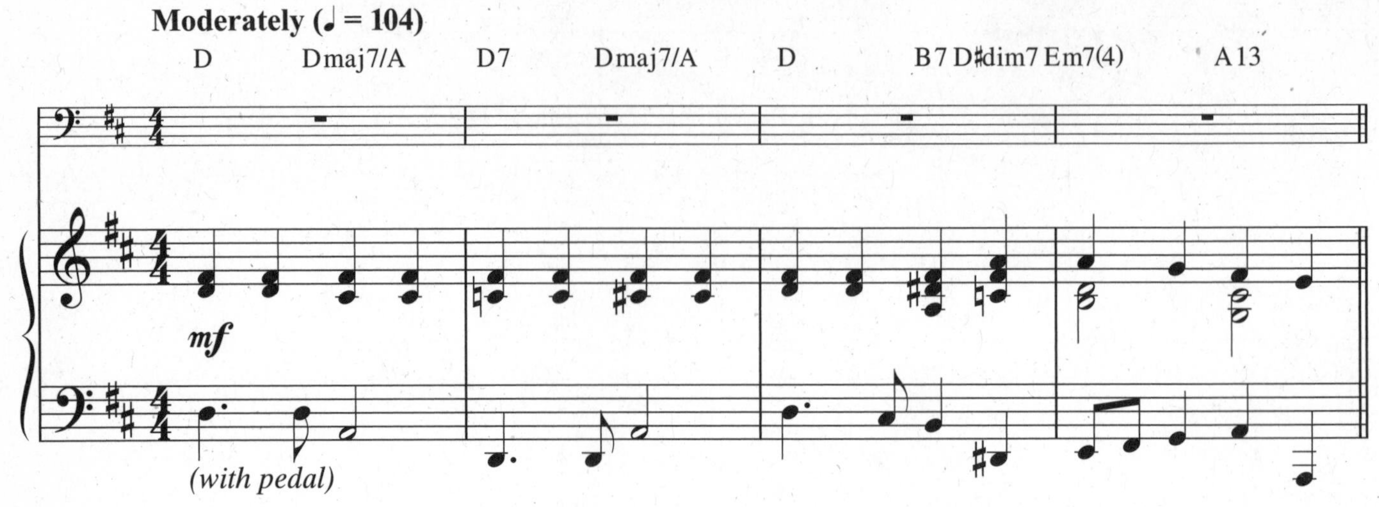

13
Bm7
Em
A7
Dmaj7
G
Em7
f
f
A
A/G
D/F♯
A
D
G6
D/A
A
19
D
Bm7
Em
A7
Dmaj7
G
Em7
f
f
A
A/G
D/F♯
A
D
G6
D/A
A7

D
Dmaj7/A
D7
Dmaj7/A
D
B7 D♯dim7 Em7(4)
A13
mf
mf
29
D
Dmaj7/A
Em7(4) A7
D
A/C♯ Bm7
D/F♯
A11
D
Bm7
F♯m7
Gmaj9 A7
D
/C♯
Bm7 F♯m7 Bm7 F♯m7
Gmaj7 A7
D
37
D
B7
Em
A7
Dmaj7
G
Em7
f
f

A
A/G
D/F♯
A
D
G6
D/A
A
43
D
B7
Em
A7
Dmaj7
G
Em7
f
f
A
A/G
D/F♯
A
D
G6
D/A
A7
D
Dmaj7/A
mf
mf
D7
Dmaj7/A
D
B7
D♯dim7
Em7(4)
A13
D
rit.

# COME, THOU LONG-EXPECTED JESUS

Music by
ROLAND H. PRICHARD

G(9)/B
Em7
Am
D7
C/G
G
C/G
G
Gmaj7
C/G
D/G
C/G
D/G
Bm7
Em
Am7
D7
C/G
G
29
Bm
Em7
Am
D7
mf
mf

G/B
Em7
Am7
D7sus
D7
G/D
D7
G/D
Am7/D
D7
G/B
Cmaj7
G/D
D7
G
mp
mp
45
Am7/G
Gmaj7
Am7/G
G/D

C G/B Am7 G B7 Em C
mf
Am Bsus B Bm Bm/D A(9)/C♯
A7 Am7 D7 D7/C
poco rit.
64
Bm
a tempo
Em7 Am D7
f
f a tempo
G/B Em7 Am7 D7sus D7 G/D
mf
mf

D7
G/D
Am7/D
D7
G/B
Cmaj7
G/D
D7
C/G
G
G/B
C
G(9)/D
D7sus
G
Am7/G
Gmaj7
Am7/G
mp
mp
G/D
C
G/B
Am7
G/B
D7sus
D7
G(9)
rit.
p

# GO, TELL IT ON THE MOUNTAIN

Traditional Spiritual

G
G/F
Em7
Cm6/E♭
C/D
G/D
D9
G
Dm
C/E
F(9)
17
G
D(9)/F♯
Em7
G/B
Am7
C/D
D7(♭9)
G
Cm6/E♭
G/D
C/D
G
D(9)/F♯
Em7
G/D
A13
A7(♯5)
A7
A/C♯
D
Em7
D9/F♯

25

G C/E G G/B B♭dim7 Am7 C/D D7

G C/E G C/D G G/F Em7 E♭7 C/D G/D D9

1. G C C♯dim7 C/D

2. G B7(♯5) C7 C♯dim7 D7 C/D D7

G C♯7(♭5) C7 B7(♯5) Am7 C/D D7(♭9) G/B C C♯dim7 C/D G

*molto rit.*

*molto rit.*

8vb

# WE THREE KINGS

Words and Music by
JOHN H. HOPKINS, JR. (1857)

**Moderately slow and tenderly (♩ = 180)**
**(𝅗𝅥. = 60 This represents the song pulse feel counted in one.)**

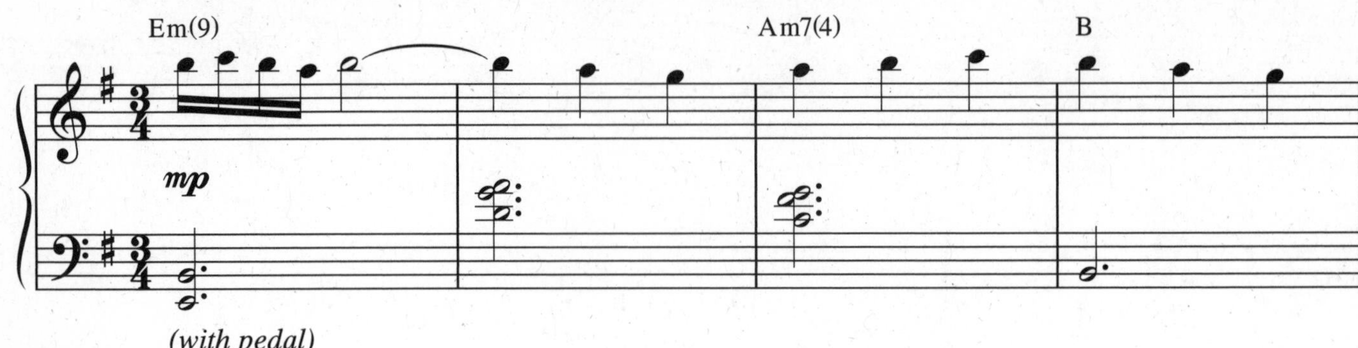

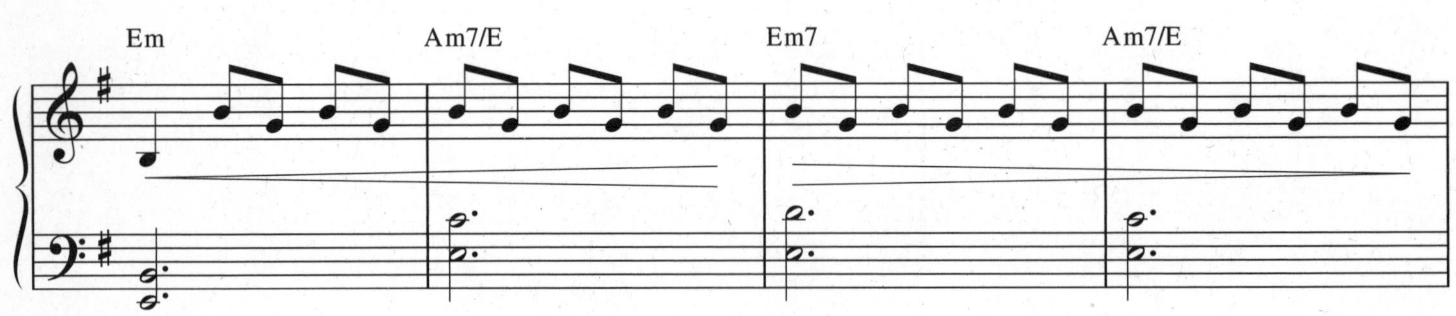

17
Em
legato
mp
B7/E
Em
B7/E
Em
D/F♯
G
F♯m7(♭5)
B7
Em
D
D7

35
G
C/G
G
mf
mf
C/G
G
Em
D/F♯
G
Am7
G/B
C
D
G
C/G
51
G
Em(9)
Am7(4)
B
f

Em(9)
F♯m7(♭5)
B7(♭9)
Em(9)
mf
63
F♯m7(♭5)/E
Em(9)
mp
mp
F♯m7(♭5)/E
Em
G

D/F♯
G
F♯m7(♭5)
B7
Em
D
D7
81
G
mf
mf
C/G
G
C/G
G

Em
D/F♯
G
Am7
G/B
C
D
G
C/G
G
Em
C
Am
D7sus
Em
F♯m7(♭5)/E
Em(9)
8va
mp
rit.
p

# IT CAME UPON THE MIDNIGHT CLEAR

Music by
RICHARD S. WILLIS

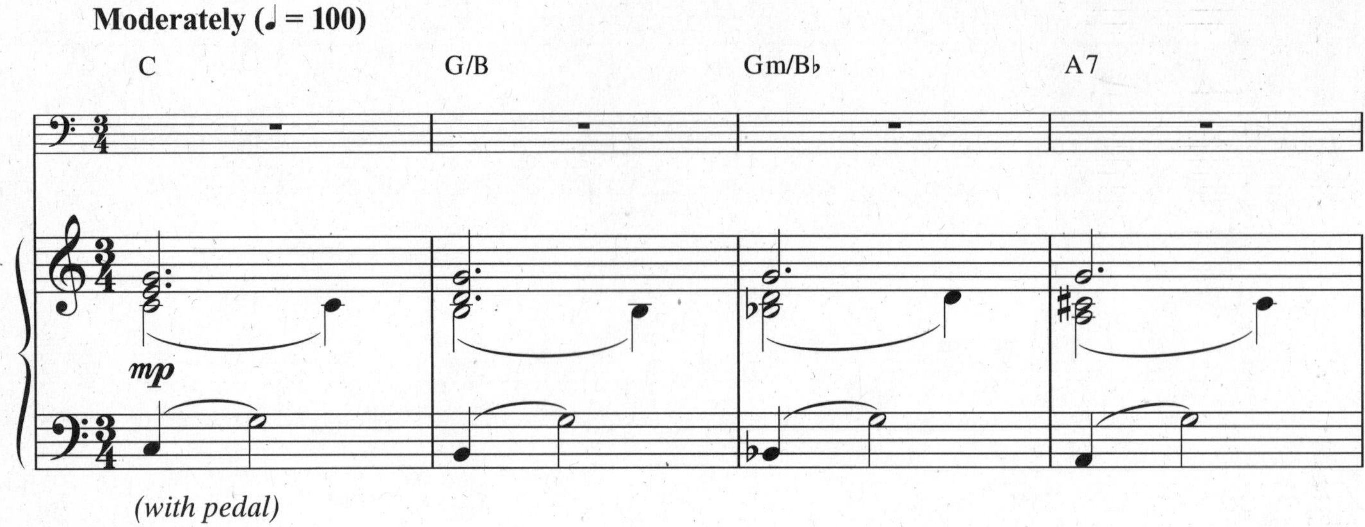

F
D7/F♯
G9sus
G7
C
A♭dim7
F/C
G9/F
C/E
Dm7
C
F
Dm7
G7
Csus
C
25
E
E7
Am
E/B
Am

G
D7
G
G7
33
C
A♭dim7
B♭/C
F/C
C
Dm7
C/E
F
G7
F/C
C
F/C
C
43
E
F♯m7
E/G♯
E7/G♯
D/A
E7/B
f
f

Am
G/B
C
Am7
G/B
Am11
G
D
Em7
D/F♯
51
G
G7
C
Em/B
B♭
F/A
F
mp
mp
C/E
Dm7
C
C/E
F
Fmaj7
G7
F
C/E
G7
C
rit.

# HARK! THE HERALD ANGELS SING

Music by
FELIX MENDELSSOHN

G Em B7/F♯ Em B Em A A7/G D/F♯ D D/A A D
21
G D/F♯ Em B Em A7 D D/A A7 D
f
f
N.C. A/G D/F♯ N.C. D/F♯ A/E Bm7 F♯m7 D/F♯ Em7 D/F♯ A11 A7
mf
29
D A D/F♯ D D/A A D/F♯ F♯m7 G D/A A D
mp
mp

A Bm7 D/A E9/G♯ F♯m7 E7/G♯ A A/C♯ E11 E7 A

37 N.C. A7/G D/F♯ A7/C♯ D D/A A Bm7 F♯m7 D/F♯ Em7 D/F♯ A11 A7

*mf*

*mf*

G Em B7/F♯ Em B7 Em A A7/G D/F♯ D D/A A/G F♯7

45 G D/F♯ Em B Em A7 D D/A A7 D

*f*

*f*

N.C. A/G D/F♯ N.C. D/F♯ A7/E Bm7 F♯m7 D/F♯ Em7 D/F♯ A11 A7 D

*mf*

*rit.*

*mp*

# JOY TO THE WORLD

Music by
GEORGE F. HANDEL

21
G7
C
F
C
F6
mf
mf
C/G
G7
C
Fmaj7
C
F6
C/G
G7
C
33
G/C
F/C
C
F6
C/G
G7
C
C/E
F
G
C
C/G
F/G
C/G
C
F/C
C
mp
mp

45
Am Am(maj7)
C/G
G7
C Cmaj7 Em7(♭5) A7
cresc. poco a poco
cresc. poco a poco
Dm
Fm G7
C F
C F6
C/G G7
C
mf
mf
57
Fmaj7
C F6
C/G G7/F
Em7(♭5) A7
Fmaj7
C F6
C/G
G7
C
f
f

# O COME, O COME, EMMANUEL

Music Adapted by
THOMAS HELMORE

Am/E
Em
D
G/D
D
D/F♯
G
F♯m7(♭5)/C
B7
Em
mf
30
D
G
Bm
Am/C
B7
Em
G/D
Cmaj7
Am7
mf
Bm7
Em
Em7/D
mp

Cmaj7
Em
8va
44
Am/C
Em6
Am/C
Em7
Em6
Am/E
Em
Am/C
Am/E
D7/E
mp
56
D
G/B
F♯m7(♭5)
B7
Em
Am/C
Em
f
f

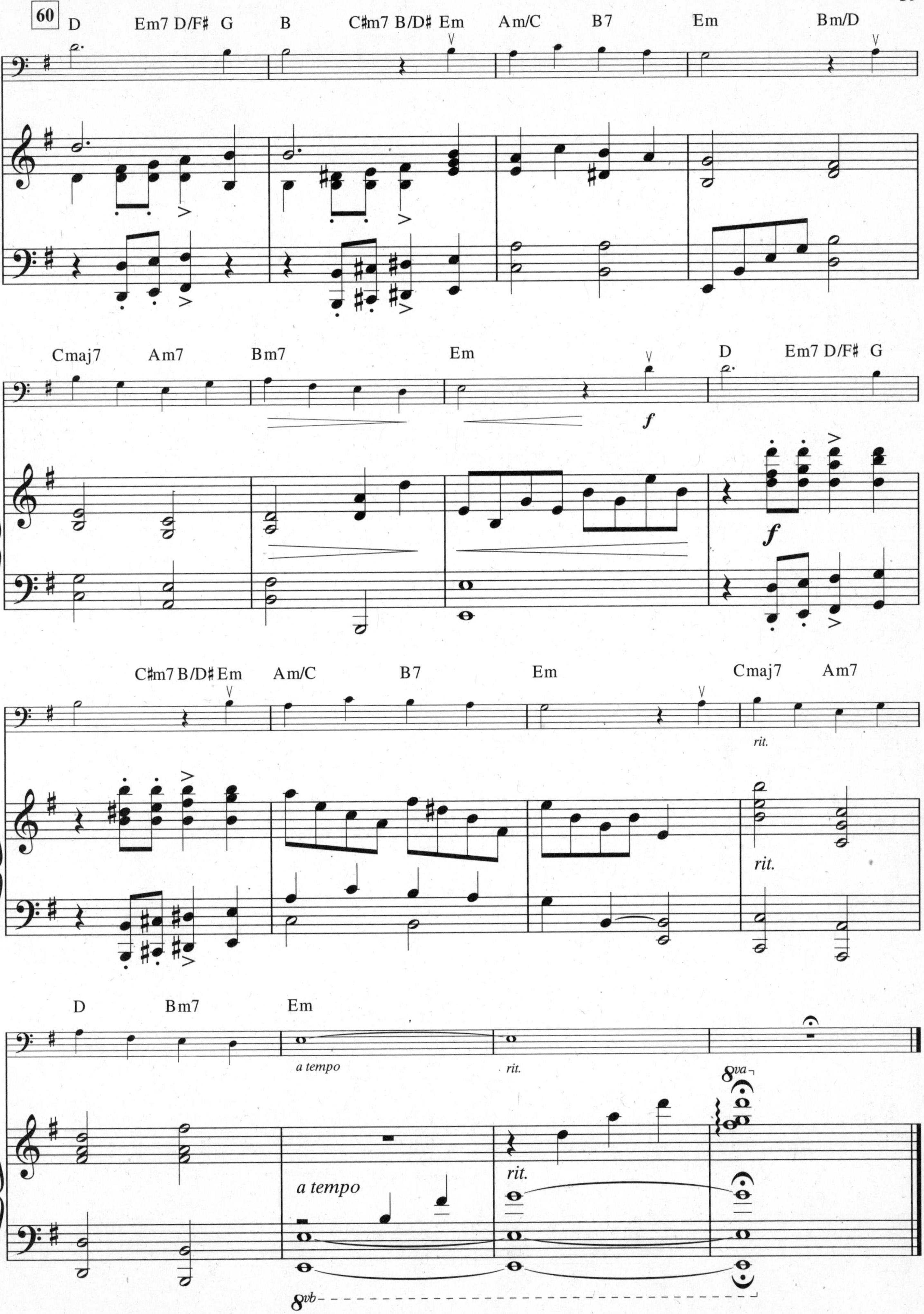
60
D Em7 D/F♯ G B C♯m7 B/D♯ Em Am/C B7 Em Bm/D
Cmaj7 Am7 Bm7 Em D Em7 D/F♯ G
f
f
C♯m7 B/D♯ Em Am/C B7 Em Cmaj7 Am7
rit.
rit.
D Bm7 Em
a tempo
rit.
8va
a tempo
rit.
8vb

# SILENT NIGHT

Words and Music by
JOSEPH MOHR and FRANZ GRUBER

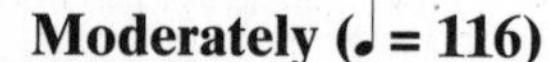


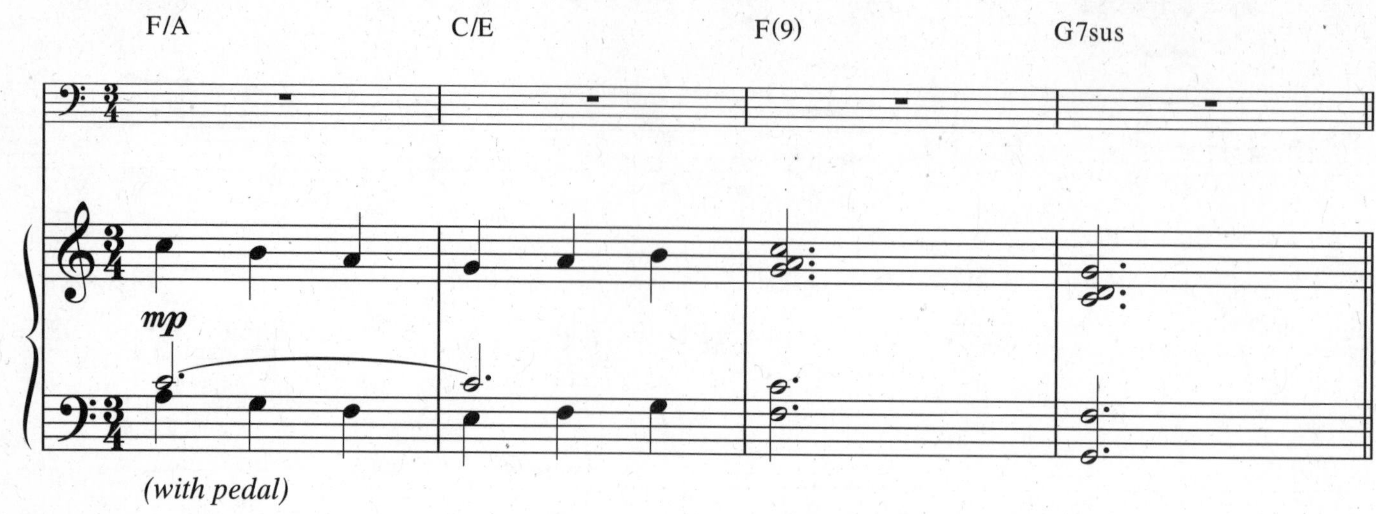

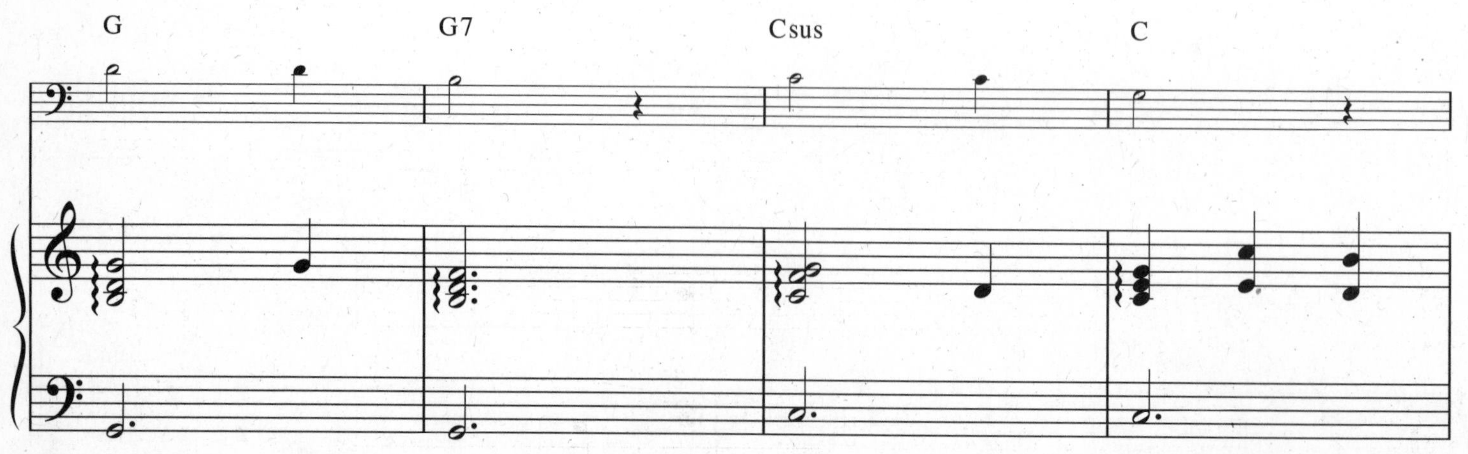

F
F/E
Dm7
G/B
C
F
F/E
Dm
C
G/B
C
21
F(9)/A
G/B
Am
C/E
C/G
G7
F/A
C/E

F(9)/G
G/B
31
C
F/C
C
mf
mf
C
F/C
C
G/B
G7
C
F
C/E
C
F

C/E
C
47
D7
G7
Am
C/E
C
G7sus
mp
mp
N.C.
Dm7
C/E
F
G7sus
f
f
F(9)
C/E
F2
G7
C
mp
p molto rit.
mp
p molto rit.

# O COME ALL YE FAITHFUL

Music by
JOHN FRANCIS WADE

17
G/B
Am
G
Am
D7
G
D/F♯
G
Em
C6
D
Em
D/F♯
G/B
f
p
21
D/A
G/B
D/C
G/B
D/A
G
D/F♯
G
D/A
G
D/F♯
G
Am
G
D/F♯
A7/E
D
D/C
G/B
Am7
G/D
D7
C(9)/E
mf
29
Dm/G
G
Dm/G
G
C/D
D
C/D
D7
C/D
D
C/D
Em7

D A7 D G/B D/F♯ G D/A A7 D D7
37
G/B Am G Am D7 Em7 D/F♯ G Em C6 D Em D/F♯ G/B
f
f
p
p
41
D/A G/B D/C G/B D/A G D/F♯ G D/A G D/F♯ G Am G D/F♯ A7/E
D D/C G/B Am7 G/D D7 C(9)/E F6/9 G6/9
mf
mf
f
f
rit.

# O LITTLE TOWN OF BETHLEHEM

Music by
LEWIS H. REDNER

13
Em Am/E Em B B/A Em D C Am B
f mp
f mp
G Edim7 G/D Dm/C C Am G/D D7 C/G G
21
Edim7 G7 C F♯m7(♭5) Am G/D D7 G G/F
E7 D/F♯ E7/G♯ Am C Cm6 G/D D7sus D7 G

29
Em7
D/F♯
G
B/D♯
F♯/C♯
B/D♯
Em7
D/F♯
G
Am
B
G
Edim7
G/D
Bm7(♭5)
C
Am
G/D
D7
G
B/D♯
G
Edim7
G/D
f
f
Dm/C
C
A/C♯
G/D
D7
C
F(9)
G
mp
mp
molto rit.
molto rit.

# THE FIRST NOEL

Traditional English Carol

C/E F G7 C G7 C G9
21 C Am G G7
f
f
C Cmaj7 G9 C G7 C Cmaj7 G9 C/E F G7 C G7
E E7/G♯
29 Am Em7 Am7 Dm7 F/G C G/B
Am G6 F C/E F G7 C G7 C
mf
poco rit.
mf
poco rit.
8vb

# WHAT CHILD IS THIS?

Old English Air

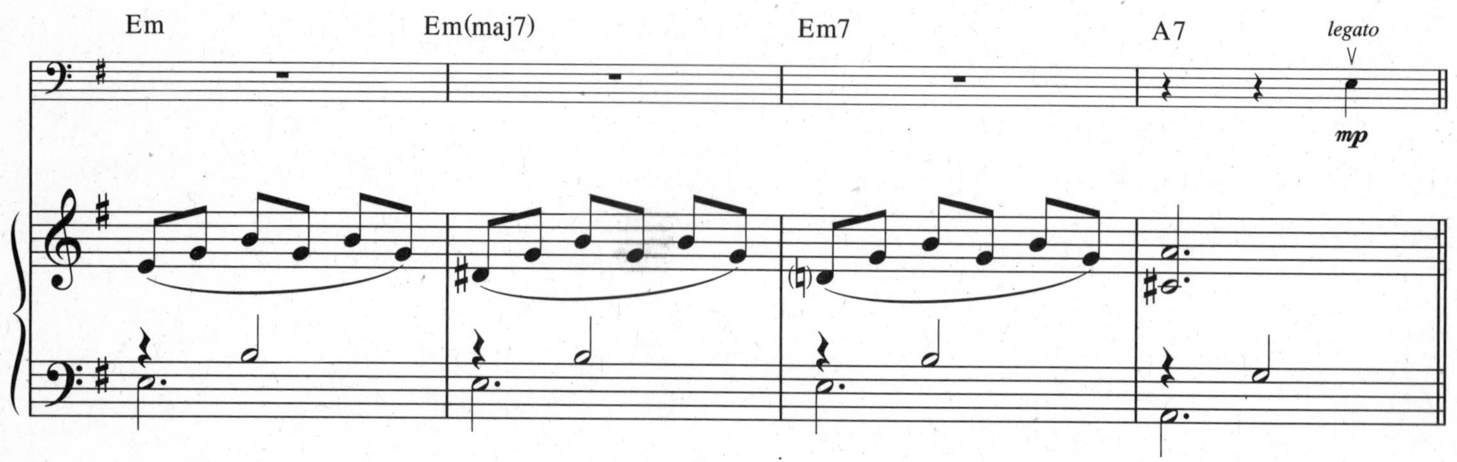

C♯m7(♭5)
F♯7
B
B/A
G6
Em
D/F♯
G
D
G
Em
A/C♯
B7
B/A
Esus
E
25
G
G/A
D
G
D♯dim7
mf
mf
Em
A(9)
B
B/A
G

E/G♯
D/A
Bm
Em
A/C♯
B
41
G6
F♯m7
Em
Em
D/F♯
G
D/F♯
D
mp
mp
Bm7
Em
A/C♯
B
Em
A7
Dmaj7
G
C

57
B
Am
Em
D/F♯
G
mf
mf
G/A
D
Bm
Em
G6
F♯7
B
B/A
G
G♯dim7
A/D
Bm
A/C♯
B/D♯
Em
B
Esus
Em
rit.
rit.

# Rolling Stone®

**INSTRUMENTAL SOLOS · VOLUME 1 & VOLUME 2**

***Rolling Stone*® Magazine's "The 500 Greatest Songs of All Time" is the ultimate celebration of the greatest rock & roll songs of all time. The editors of *Rolling Stone*® called on a five-star jury of singers, musicians, producers, industry figures, critics and, of course, songwriters. The 172 voters, who included Brian Wilson, Joni Mitchell and Wilco's Jeff Tweedy, nominated 2,103 songs in virtually every pop-music genre of the past half-century and beyond, from Hank Williams to OutKast. The results were tabulated according to a weighted point system. Alfred is proud to introduce an impressive new instrumental play-along collections that make songs from the *Rolling Stone 500* playable to music makers everywhere!**

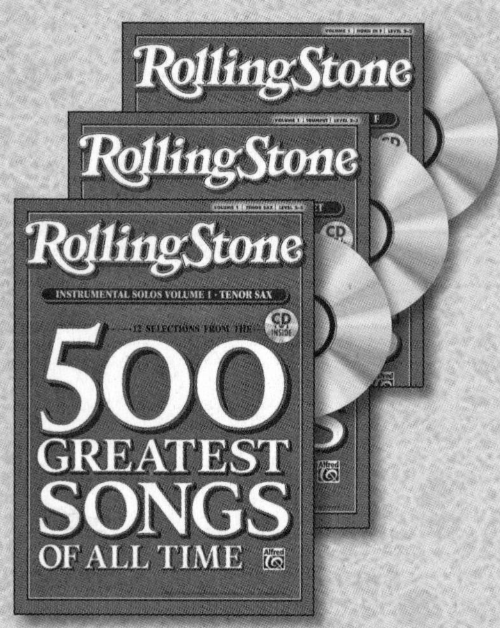


### Selections from *Rolling Stone*® Magazine's 500 Greatest Songs of All Time: Instrumental Solos, Vol. 1 & 2

Each book contains a carefully edited part that is appropriate for Level 2-3 players, and a fully orchestrated accompaniment CD that includes both demo and play-along tracks for each song. Vol. 1 titles: Both Sides, Now • Desperado • Everyday People • A Hard Day's Night • Honky Tonk Women • Moondance • (We're Gonna) Rock Around the Clock • Soul Man • When a Man Loves a Woman • and more. Vol. 2 titles: Blueberry Hill • Dancing Queen • Hotel California • How Deep Is Your Love • I Got You (I Feel Good) • In the Midnight Hour • (I Can't Get No) Satisfaction • Spirit in the Sky • You Send Me • and more.

| VOL. 1 | VOL. 2 | | |
|---|---|---|---|
| (00-30335) | (00-30842) | Flute (Book & CD) | $12.95 |
| (00-30338) | (00-30845) | Clarinet (Book & CD) | $12.95 |
| (00-30341) | (00-30848) | Alto Sax (Book & CD) | $12.95 |
| (00-30344) | (00-30851) | Tenor Sax (Book & CD) | $12.95 |
| (00-30347) | (00-30854) | Trumpet (Book & CD) | $12.95 |
| (00-30350) | (00-30857) | Horn in F (Book & CD) | $12.95 |
| (00-30353) | (00-30860) | Trombone (Book & CD) | $12.95 |
| (00-30359) | (00-30866) | Violin (Book & CD) | $14.95 |
| (00-30362) | (00-30869) | Viola (Book & CD) | $14.95 |
| (00-30365) | (00-30872) | Cello (Book & CD) | $14.95 |
| (00-30356) | (00-30863) | Piano Accompaniment (Book & CD) | $14.95 |

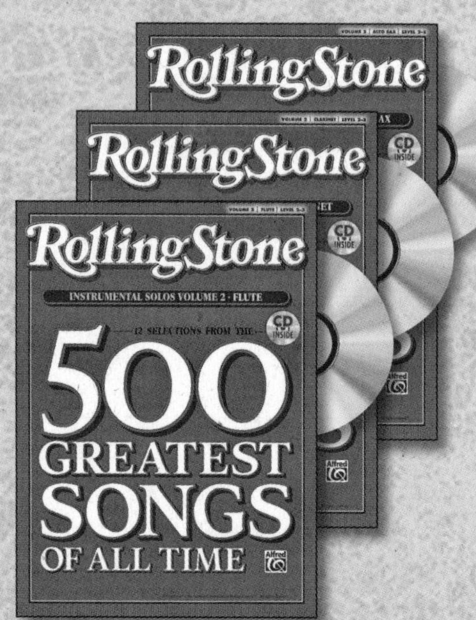